hedgerow

SIMONE GOODING

LAUREL

CHAMOMILE

DAMSON

Tuva Publishing

www.tuvapublishing.com

Address Merkez Mah. Cavusbasi Cad. No:71
Cekmekoy - Istanbul 34782 / Turkey
Tel: +9 0216 642 62 62

Hedgerow

First Print 2022 / January

All Global Copyrights Belong To
Tuva Tekstil ve Yayıncılık Ltd.

Content Sewing

Editor in Chief Ayhan DEMİRPEHLİVAN
Project Editor Kader DEMİRPEHLİVAN
Designer Simone GOODING
Technical Editor Leyla ARAS
Graphic Designers Simone GOODING, Ömer ALP,
Abdullah BAYRAKÇI, Tarık TOKGÖZ, Yunus GÜLDOĞAN
Photograph and Illustrations Simone GOODING

ISBN 978-605-7834-65-2

 TuvaYayincilik   TuvaPublishing
 TuvaYayincilik   TuvaPublishing

Contents

stitch and dress all the beautiful Hedgerow Dolls...
with all their outfits and accessories

hedgerow

Let's explore ...

... the enchanting world of the

hedgerow dolls

created by artist and illustrator Simone Gooding.

Containing a mixture of charming illustrations and photographs to help bring to life, their little Hedgerow community. In this craft book you will find a variety of outfits and accessories to stitch, knit and make.

Travel along through their woodland home as they gather all they need to explore the leafy world that surrounds them.

You will find a Felt Bushel for collecting the Knitted Apples, Dungarees with Applique Felt Rabbit Pockets, Fallow Deer Knitted Hat, a Felt Fox Satchel, Knitted Bobble Hat with Felt Robin and many more.

With 100% wool hand dyed felt Hedgerow Dolls, and over 20 original knitted, felt and fabric outfits and accessories, 'Hedgerow' provides all the inspiration and know-how needed to bring these beautiful dolls to life.

100% wool hand dyed felt

I have been using Winterwood 100% wool hand dyed felt for many years now. It is very strong but also wonderfully soft so performs beautifully every time. In this book I have referenced names from their colour chart making it easier for you to use the exact same colours that I have used, if you so choose. I highly recommend you use very high quality wool felt, poor quality or synthetic felt will not withstand the small seam allowance, tight turning of pieces and firm stuffing required.

buttons

For many years now I have been collecting vintage buttons. I just love to use vintage buttons, they have such wonderful colours, patterns and designs. My favourites are made of Bakelite Plastic from the 1940's and 50's. I have used a few from my collection in this book.

English glass doll making eyes

I just love this product! They are beautifully handmade and are very easy to use. They are jet black and have a little sheen on them which help to bring your toy animal/doll to life.

Jamieson's of Shetland yarn

I have been designing little sweaters, scarves, and hats for my toys for many years now. They are usually quite small in size so a gently fine yarn is needed. Once I found Jamieson's of Shetland's Spindrift I have not looked back. It is a 2ply jumper fingering-weight yarn, which is equivalent to a 4ply. It performs beautifully for small knitted items and has a wonderful, large range of colours in lovely muted, heathered tones.

setting the eyes

1 Mark the position of the eyes with pins.

2 Cut a long piece of Gutterman Upholstery Thread and thread it through the metal loop at the back of the eye.

4 Take the needle off the thread and thread the needle again with only one length of the thread. Push the needle up through the stuffing and out of the face right next to one side of the eye. Repeat with the remaining thread on the other side of the eye.

3 Thread a long doll making needle with both ends of the thread, and push the needle through the front of the face at the position of the first pin. Bring the needle out in the stuffing at the neck.

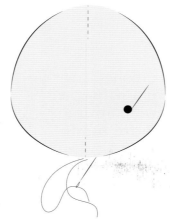

5 Take the two lengths of thread that are poking out on either side of the eye and tie a triple knot, pulling it tight so the knot is hidden behind the back of the eye.

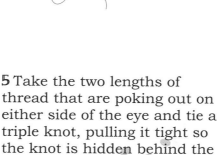

6 Now thread the needle again with one of the lengths of thread and push the needle back in next to the eye and out through the stuffing in the neck. Repeat with the remaining thread.

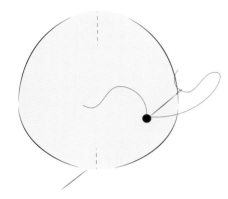

7 Tie a triple knot in the stuffing in the neck a few times until the eye is secure. Repeat steps 1-7 again with the remaining eye.

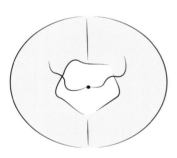

hedgerow dolls

head

1 Fold one head piece in half along the fold line down the centre of the head, machine stitch along both gusset seams, repeat with the remaining head piece.

2 Open out the two headpieces and with right sides of the heads facing and the top and bottom gussets matching, stitch around the outer edge of the head, leaving open at the bottom where indicated.

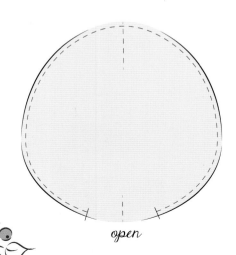

open

3 Turn the head right side out and stuff very firmly. The head circumference should measure approx. 25cm (10").

25cm (10")

4 Stitch in approx. 1cm (1/2") from each side of the head opening.

5 Mark the position for the eyes with pins as indicated. Following the eye setting instructions on page 12, attach the English glass eyes.

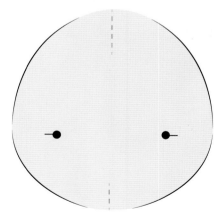

6 Using four strands of black embroidery thread, stitch an eyelash on the outer side of each eye.

body

1 Machine stitch all the way around the two body pieces, leaving open where indicated at the bottom.

2 Turn the body right side out and stuff very firmly, making sure to stuff the neck very firmly. The body circumference should measure approx. 19cm (7.5").

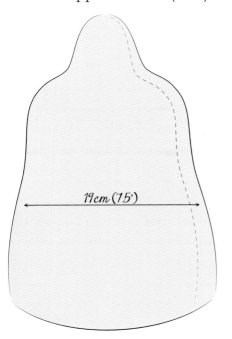

legs

1 Stitch the legs all the way around, leaving open at the top where indicated. Turn right side out and stuff the leg very firmly up to the 'gather line'. Using matching embroidery thread to the felt, gather by hand around the leg along the gather line. Pull up the gathers and fasten off.

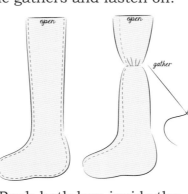

2 Push both legs inside the opening at the bottom of the body until they are firm, pin them in place. Using two strands of matching embroidery thread, hand stitch the legs to the body, tucking under a tiny raw edge as you stitch.

3 Make a small indent with your finger in the opening in the head and push the neck of the body inside the head, hold the head on with pins while you stitch the head in place, tucking under the raw edge of the felt as you go.

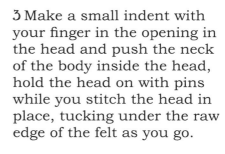
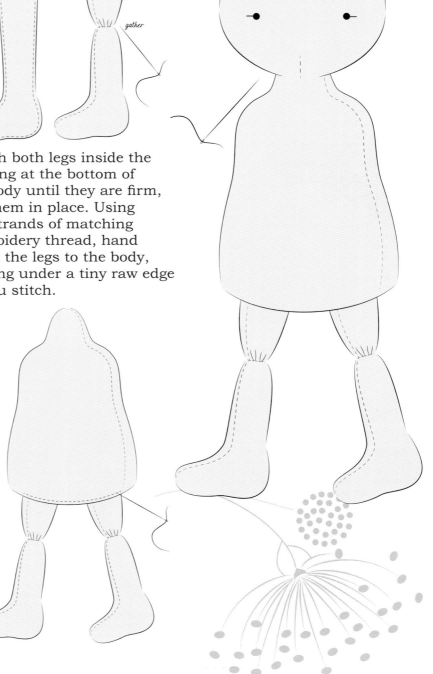

arms

1 Stitch the arms all the way around, leaving open where indicated, turn right side out and stuff the arms firmly in the hands and up to the gather line. (Leave the top part of each arm unstuffed).

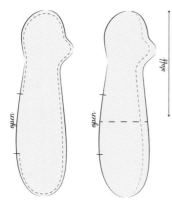

2 Place a pin to hold the stuffing in place while you close the opening.

4 Pin the arms to each side of the body just under the head with the thumbs facing forward. With two strands of Gutermann Upholstery Thread and a long doll making needle, stitch right through one arm through the body and out the other side of the other arm, keep going through in this fashion many times until the arms are firm, fasten off.

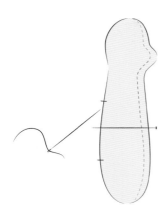

3 Using matching embroidery thread to the felt, gather by hand around the arm along the gather line. Pull up the gathers and fasten off.

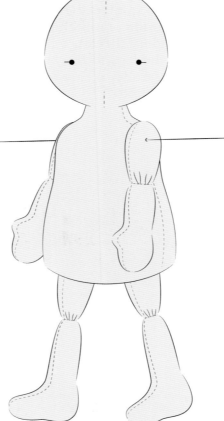

hair

1 Mark with pins the centre front of the head gusset seam and also place a pin in the back of the gusset seam.

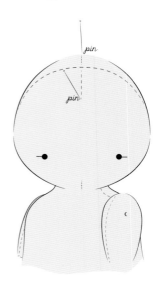

2 Choose desired three colours of yarn for the hair. You will need 90cm (35.5") lengths. 60 of each colour. (180 strands in total)

3 Take 20 stands of each colour and lay them on a table in a random fashion.

4 Fold them in half to find the centre.

5 Place the centre of the first bundle of yarn behind the first pin in the centre front of the head gusset. Using two strands of matching thread, stitch the hair in place along the head gusset seam.

pin

pin

6 Measure down each side of the head approx. 8cm (3¼") and place a pin in the head side seam. Gently pull the yarn down to this mark and stitch the yarn to the side of the head.

stitch *pin* *pin* *stitch*

7 Now stitch the hair around the back of the head in a curved fashion, and up to the other side.

stitch

8 Take a second bundle of yarn with 20 strands of each colour, randomly placed together. Find the centre of the bundle, pin and stitch the centre of the bundle to the centre front of the head gusset, on top of the first bundle. (Stitch to the top head gusset only, not at the sides and back)

9 Now repeat with the final bundle of 20.

10 Now style the hair in any way that you choose:
 - Plait down the centre back.
 - divide into two plaits.
 - Take a small amount on top and tie, leaving the remainder out and long.
 - Divide into two and tie in low pigtails.

11 Tie the hair with matching yarn. Once you have styled the hair as desired, trim the ends to be neat.

Chamomile

short sleeve blouse

YOU WILL NEED

- 45cm x 32cm (18" x 12.5") fabric for blouse

- 15cm (6") piece of thin elastic

- Sewing machine thread to match the fabric

- x2 Small vintage/novelty buttons

- Perle thread for the button loops

- General sewing supplies

* 5mm (¼") seam allowance included

* templates on page 112

bodice

1 With right sides together, place the bodice fronts together and machine stitch all the way around, leaving open where indicated along the bottom edge. Clip the corners and curves and turn right side out and press.

2 Turn under the raw hem edge and press. Top stitch it in place.

3 Take two of the bodice back pieces and with right sides together, machine stitch all the way around, leaving open where indicated along the bottom edge. Clip the corners and curves, turn right side out and press.

3.

4 Turn under the raw hem edge and press. Top stitch in place.

5 With the two remaining bodice back pieces, machine stitch down the centre back seam, open out and press. Using a matching Perle thread, stitch two small button loop as indicated. Now machine stitch the rest in the same way as for steps three and four.

open

open

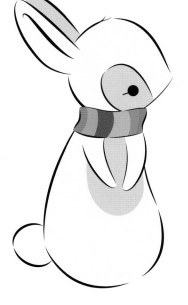

open

6 Hand stitch one bodice back to the bodice front along the shoulder seams.

sleeves

1 Press under a neat hem on each sleeve approx. 3cm (1¼") wide.

2 Top stitch all the way across the hem. Stitch another row of stitching approx. 1.5cm (½") under the first row to make the elastic casing.

3 Machine gather around the curved edge of each sleeve, between the arrows.

gather

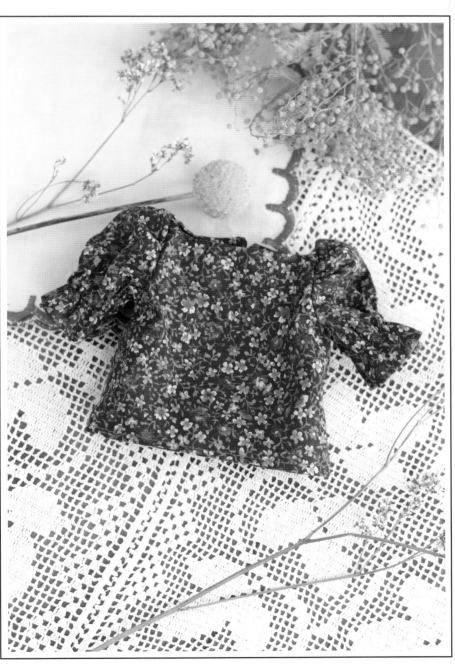

4 Open out the bodice, with right sides together, stitch each sleeve to the underarm of the bodice stopping at the indicated 'X', adjusting gathers in the sleeve to fit as you go.

5 Cut approx. 7.5cm (3") long piece of elastic. Thread it through the casing on the end of a safety pin.

elastic

6 Top stitch the end of the elastic just inside the end of the casing. Pull the remainder of the elastic through the rest of the casing, top stitch the remaining end in the casing, trim the end of the elastic if needed.

7 With right sides together, machine stitch down the sleeve seam and hand stitch down the side seam of the bodice.

7.

stitch   stitch

8 Turn the blouse right side out and stitch two tiny vintage/novelty buttons to the bodice back opposite the button loops.

8.

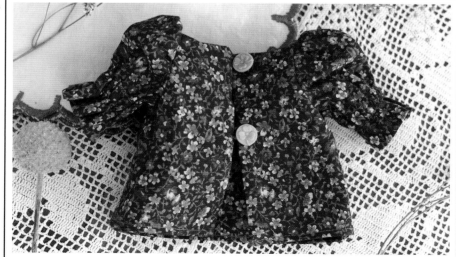

dungarees

YOU WILL NEED

. 47cm x 33cm (18.5"x 13") fabric for dungarees

. 10cm x 8cm (4"x 3") 'Ecru wool felt for rabbit applique

. Embroidery thread to match the felt

. Embroidery thread for flowers

. Black embroidery thread for rabbit eyes

. Sewing machine thread to match the fabric

. x2 Small vintage/novelty buttons

. Tiny applique pins (optional)

. General sewing supplies

* 5mm (¼") seam allowance included

* templates on page 116

dungarees

1 Cut four pocket pieces from fabric. Take two of the pocket pieces and lay them down on your work table with the curved edge facing the middle.

2 Using small scraps of 100% wool, hand dyed felt, cut out two rabbit applique pieces. Using the placement guide, position the rabbits in line with the curved edge of each pocket. Using two strands of matching embroidery thread, blanket stitch around the outer edge of both rabbits. Use a contrasting colour thread to hand stitch long back stitches through the centre of the ears.

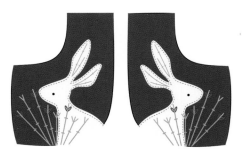

4 Using four strands of black embroidery thread, stitch one French Knot for the eye of each rabbit.

5 With right sides together, machine stitch around the inner curved edge and the outer curved edge of each pocket, leaving open where indicated. Turn the pockets right side out and press well.

stitch

stitch

3 Using two strands of green embroidery thread, stitch long backstitches in place randomly on each pocket to form the stems of the flowers. Using two strands of a contrasting thread, stitch a few random Lazy Daisy flowers and then another contrasting thread to stitch a few backstitch flowers.

6 Pin the pockets as indicated to the front of the dungaree pieces, hand stitch around the outer curved edge only of each pocket, leaving open at the inner curved edge.

7 With right sides together, stitch the dungaree fronts along the gusset seam only, now repeat with the two dungaree backs.

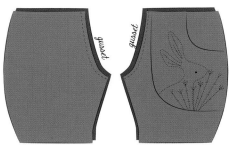

8 Turn up a small, neat hem on the bottom of the legs of the dungarees and machine stitch in place.

waistband

1 Cut two strips of fabric for the waistband that measure 5½" x 1" (14cm x 2½cm). With right sides together, machine stitch one waistband to the top of the dungaree fronts along the top edge. Press the band up and over to the wrong side.

2 Hand stitch the waistband in place on the wrong side, tucking under the raw edge as you stitch. Press well. Repeat with the remaining waistband piece and the dungaree backs.

3 With right sides together, machine stitch the dungarees down the side seams and the inner leg seam. Turn right side out and press.

bib

1 With right side together, machine stitch around the outer edge of the bib pieces, leaving open where indicated. Clip corners, turn right side out and press well. Hand stitch the opening closed.

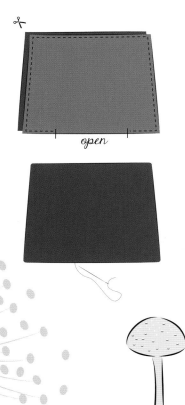

2 Hand stitch one long edge of the bib to the front inside edge of the waistband.

straps

1 Using a 1" bias tape maker, make two straps that measure 2"x 7" (5cm x 18cm). Tuck in the raw ends and top stitch each strap.

2"x 7" (5cm x 18cm)

2 Hand stitch one end of each strap to the inside top edge of the bib.

black snap

3 Stitch one side of a small black snap/ press stud to the top side of the other end of the strap and the remaining side of the snap to the inside of the waistband at the back to fasten.

4 Stitch two tiny vintage/ novelty buttons in place on the top of the bib.

knitted bobble hat

* Beginning at the band edge and using the colour for the band, cast on 76 stitches.

1 Knit 1, Purl 1, - 4 rows

Break off Band Colour.

2 Join on Pink * Beginning with a knit row, st st 2 rows.

3 Join on White, beginning with a knit row st st 2 rows. **

4 Stocking Stitch 12 rows following the stripe sequence between the *-**

5 Continuing the stripe sequence, knit 2, knit 2 together to the end of the row - 57 stitches.

6 Stocking Stitch 3 rows.

7 Knit 2 together at each end of next and every alternate row until 2 stitches remain.

8 Cut the yarn from the ball, leaving a long length. Thread a bodkin with the length and thread it through the 2 stitches on the knitting needle, pull gently until firm.

* Block the piece by laying a piece of kitchen towel over it and using a cool iron to steam. Allow the piece to dry.

making up

1 Thread the long length of yarn on to a bodkin. Mattress stitch the row ends together all the way down to the band. Weave in the ends of any remaining yarn. Fasten off.

robin

❧ YOU WILL NEED ❧

. 10cm x 5cm (4" x 2")
 'Bloodwood' wool felt
 for robin body

. 10cm x 4cm (4"x 1.5")
 'Nutmeg' wool felt for
 robin gusset

. 6cm x 4cm (2.5" x 1.5")
 'Mallee' wool felt for
 robin crest and wings

. Embroidery thread to
 match the felt

. Black embroidery thread

. White embroidery thread

. Toy fill

. General sewing supplies

templates on page 120

1 Take one wing and stitch it in place on one body piece through the centre, using two strands of embroidery thread. Repeat with the remaining wing and body piece.

2 Using two strands of matching embroidery thread, to the body colour, take one body piece and blanket stitch the head gusset in place from the beak end up and over the top of the head. Repeat with the remaining body piece.

3 Blanket stitch one side of the body piece to the body gusset, matching the symbols.

4 Repeat with the remaining body piece on the other side of the body gusset, stop just before you get to the end.

5 Stuff the robin until firm, continue stitching to the end. Fasten off.

6 Using four strands of white embroidery thread, stitch two French knots in place for the eyes. Now using two strands of black embroidery thread, stitch a small backstitch in place over the top of the French Knot as a small pupil.

7 7. Using two strands of black embroidery thread, stitch over and over on the pointed end of the body to form the beak.

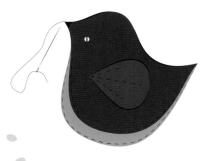

8 Stitch the little robin to the pointy end of the bobble hat.

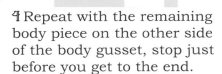

vest

vest

-YOU WILL NEED-

. 18cm x 18cm (7" x 7") fabric for vest

. 18cm x 18cm (7" x 7") 'Oak' wool felt for vest

. Sewing machine thread to match the felt

. Contrasting embroidery thread

. General sewing supplies

* 5mm (¼") seam allowance included

* templates on page 114

1 Using Laurel's Dress Bodice Front pattern piece. Cut one fabric and one felt for the back of the Vest.

2 Cut two Vest Front pieces from fabric and two from felt.

3 With right sides together, stitch all the way around the two Vest Back pieces, leaving open where indicated along the bottom edge. Clip corners and curves, turn right side out and press well. Hand stitch the opening closed.

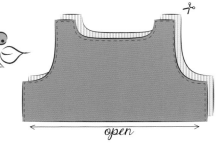

open

4 Repeat step three with the two sets of Vest Front pieces.

5 Hand stitch the shoulder seams on the two fronts to the shoulder seams of the back piece.

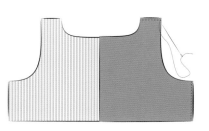

6 Hand stitch down the side seams.

7 Fold the front top corner of the vest over to reveal the lining. Using a contrasting colour thread, hand stitch a larger 'X' in each corner to hold in place.

knitted leg warmers

leg warmers

Beginning at the band edge and using the colour for the band, cast on 26 stitches.

1 Knit 1, Purl 1, - 4 rows

Break off Band Colour.

2 Join on Pink * Beginning with a knit row, st st 2 rows.

3 Join on White, beginning with a knit row st st 2 rows. **

4 Stocking Stitch 26 rows following the stripe sequence between the *-**

Break off Pink and White.

5 Join on Band Colour, Knit 1, Purl 1, - 4 rows

6 Cast off Knit Wise.

* Block the piece by laying a piece of kitchen towel over it and using a cool iron to steam. Allow the piece to dry.

making up

1 Thread the length of yarn on to a bodkin. Mattress stitch the row ends together all the way down to the band. Weave in the ends of any remaining yarn. Fasten off.

peg doll

peg doll

YOU WILL NEED

- . 12cm x 12cm (5"x 5") 'Mallee' wool felt for the cape

- . Embroidery thread to match the felt

- . x1 6cm (2 1/3") tall wooden peg doll

- . Contrasting Perle thread

- . x2 4mm seed beads with 1.8mm hole

- . Black marker pen

- . General sewing supplies

*templates on page 120

1 1. Using two strands of matching embroidery thread, blanket stitch all the way around the inner part of the peg doll cape as indicated.

blanket stitch

2 Fold the piece in half. Using two strands of matching embroidery thread, blanket stitch down the centre back seam of the cape.

blanket stitch

3 Gather by hand around the neck area of the cape as indicated, place the cape on the wooden peg doll, pull the

gathers firmly and fasten in the centre front.

gather

4 Using two strands of contrasting Perle cotton thread, wrap a long length around the neck of the doll and tie firmly in the centre front.

5 Thread a 4mm seed bead with a 1.8mm hole on to the ends of the Perle cotton thread and tie a knot in the end of the thread.

6 Using a thin black marker pen, draw two tiny oval shaped eyes in place on the front of the doll. Place the doll in the pocket of Chamomile's dungarees.

rabbit backpack

backpack

1 Cut out two tiny dots from black felt for the eyes. Place them as indicated on the face of the rabbit. Using two strands of black embroidery thread, blanket stitch around the tiny dots. (You could also stitch French Knots for the eyes using 4 strands of black embroidery thread, if you prefer.) Stitch long stitches for the eye lashes, nose and mouth as illustrated.

2 With right sides together, stitch all the way around the backpack, leaving open where indicated at the face end.

3 Clip the corners and curves and turn the piece right side out and press.

4 Bring together one side with one rectangle end and hand stitch them together, repeat until all four sides are stitched.)

stitch   stitch

stitch   stitch

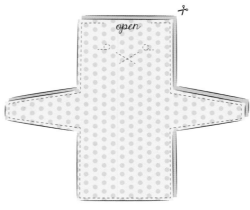

open

3 Tuck each ear with the pink side facing forward into the opening in the backpack. Hand stitch the opening closed making sure to catch the ends of the ears in the stitching.

2 Fold each strap in half lengthwise and top stitch.

7.5" x 1" (19cm x 2.5cm)

3 Hand stitch one end of each strap to the top of the back of the backpack. Stitch the remaining end of both straps to the bottom of the back of the backpack.

ears

1 Cut two ears from pale pink felt and two from the same colour felt as the backpack. Place them together in pairs each pair having one pale pink and one body colour. Machine stitch all the way around each ear leaving the bottom straight edge open, turn right side out.

straps

1 Cut two straps from wool felt that measure 7.5"x 1" (19cm x 2.5cm)

open

2 Make a little fold in the straight end of each ear and hold with a small stitch.

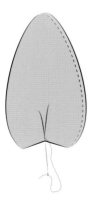

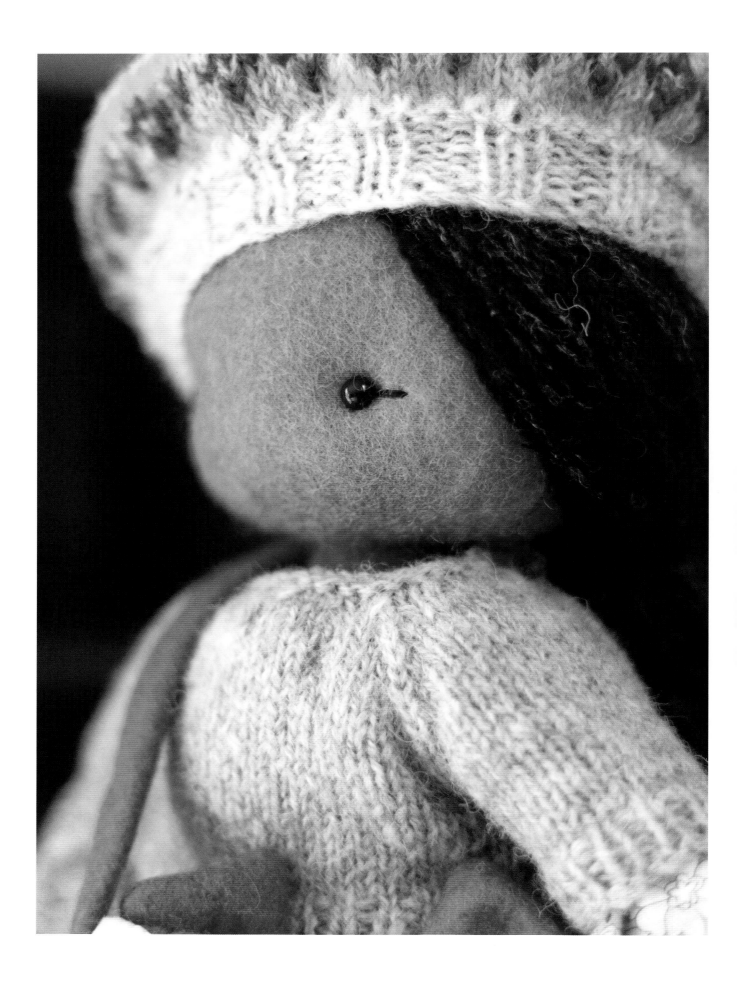

Laurel

dress

YOU WILL NEED

. 50cm x 40cm (20"x 16") fabric for dress

. Sewing machine thread to match the fabric

. x1 Small vintage/novelty button

. Perle thread for the button loop

. General sewing supplies

* 5mm (¼") seam allowance included

* templates on page 114

bodice

1 With right sides together, place the bodice fronts together and machine stitch all the way around, leaving open where indicated along the bottom edge. Clip the corners and curves and turn right side out and press.

2 Take two of the bodice back pieces and with right sides together, machine stitch all the way around, leaving open where indicated along the bottom edge. Clip the corners and curves, turn right side out and press.

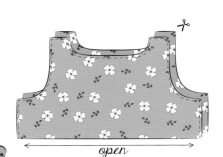

open

open

3 With the two remaining bodice back pieces, machine stitch down the centre back seam, open out and press. Using a matching Perle thread, stitch one small button loop towards the top. Now machine stitch the rest in the same way as for step two. Repeat with the remaining bodice back.

open

4 Hand stitch one bodice back to the bodice front along the shoulder seams.

sleeves

1 Machine gather around the curved edge of each sleeve, between the arrows.

gather

2 Open out the bodice, with right sides together, stitch each sleeve to the underarm of the bodice stopping approx. at the indicated 'X', adjusting gathers in the sleeve to fit as you go.

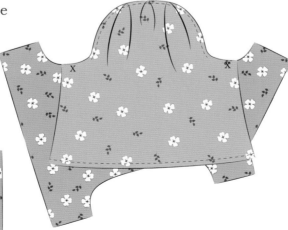

3 Press under a neat hem on the cuff edge of each sleeve. Stitch in place and press.

4 With right sides together, machine stitch down the sleeve seam and hand stitch down the side seam of the bodice.

stitch *stitch*

2 With right sides together, machine stitch down the centre back seam of the skirt, press.

3 Machine gather around the top raw edge of the skirt.

gather

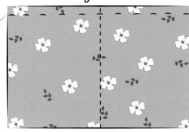

skirt

1 Cut a piece of fabric for the skirt that measures 20cm x 50cm (8"x 20")

20 x 50 cm (8 x 20 inches)

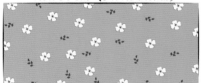

4 With right sides together, and the centre back seam of the skirt facing the back, hand stitch the gathered edge of the skirt to the raw edge of the bodice, adjusting the gathers as you go.

5 Press under a neat hem on the skirt and stitch in place, press.

6 Turn the dress right side out and stitch a tiny vintage/novelty button to the bodice back opposite the button loop.

stitch

knitted sweater

sweater

The sweater is worked in the following order: sleeve, front, sleeve, back.

Always cast on each section, on the needle with the worked sections already on it.

first sleeve

* Beginning at the cuff edge, cast on 26 stitches.

1 k1, p1 x4 rows for the band

2 Beginning with a purl row, st-st 6 rows.

3 Cut yarn from the work, leaving a 13cm (5") tail for stitching up later, leave work on the needle.

front

* Beginning at the bottom edge, cast on 36 stitches.

1 k1, p1 x4 rows for the band.

2 Beginning with a purl row, st-st 6 rows.

3 Cut yarn from the work, leaving a 13cm (5") tail for stitching up later, leave work on the needle.

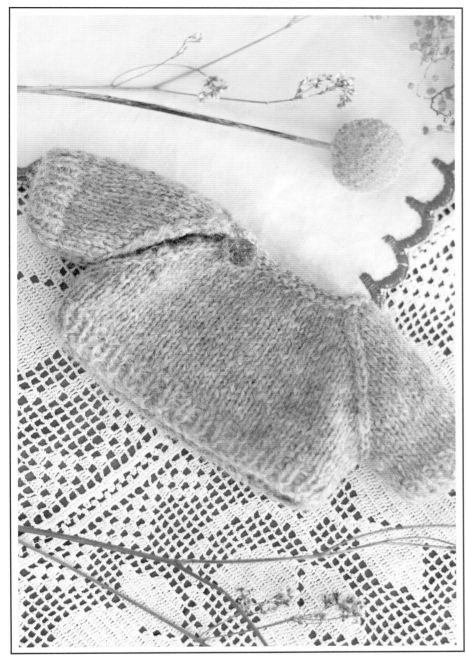

Row 5: Purl

Row 6: K1, SSK, k17, CDD, k28, CDD, k18, CDD, k27, k2tog, k1 – 97 stitches

Row 7: Purl

Row 8: K1, SSK, k15, CDD, k26, CDD, k16, CDD, k25, k2tog, k1 – 89 stitches

Row 9: Purl

Row 10: K1, SSK, k13, CDD, k24, CDD, k14, CDD, k23, k2tog, k1 – 81 stitches

Row 11: Purl

Row 12: K1, SSK, k11, CDD, k22, CDD, k12, CDD, k21, k2tog, k1 – 73 stitches

Row 13: Purl

Row 14: K1, SSK, k9, CDD, k20, CDD, k10, CDD, k19, k2tog, k1 – 65 stitches

Row 15: Purl

Row 16: K1, SSK, k7, CDD, k18, CDD, k8, CDD, k17, k2tog, k1 – 57 stitches

Row 17: P1, p2tog, to the end of the row

Row 18: Purl

Cast off knitwise.

Block the piece by laying a piece of kitchen towel over it and using a cool iron to steam.

second sleeve

Repeat in the same way as for the first sleeve.

back

Repeat in the same way as for the front. – don't cut the yarn.

* There should be 124 stitches on the needle.

decreasing

Row 1: P35, p2tog, p24, p2tog, p34, p2tog, p25 – 121 stitches

Row 2: K1, SSK, k21, CDD, k32, CDD, k22, CDD, k31, k2tog, k1 –113 stitches

Row 3: Purl

Row 4: K1, SSK, k19, CDD, k30, CDD, k20, CDD, k29, k2tog, k1 – 105 stitches

making up

1 Beginning with the front facing you, mattress stitch up the left side seam and along the underarm seam. Weave in the ends of the yarn.

2 Mattress stitch up the side seam approx. 3cm (1¼") on the right side and fasten off. Weave in the ends of the yarn.

3 Beginning at the sleeve end, stitch along the underarm until you reach the side seam fasten off, weave in the ends of the yarn.

button loop

Finger knit (or crochet) a 3cm (1¼) long chain. With the back of the sweater facing you, stitch the ends of the button loop to the top left corner of the neckline. Stitch a small button in place along the neckline towards the back.

apron

YOU WILL NEED

. 66cm x 30cm (26"x 12") pale grey linen

. Small scraps of 'Mallee' 'Daintree' 'Ecru' and 'Bulloak' for the toadstool applique

. Embroidery thread to match the felt

. White embroidery thread

. Sewing machine thread to match the linen

. General sewing supplies

* 5mm (¼") seam allowance included

* applique templates on page 126

apron

For the apron cut the following:
  x1 piece that measures - 16"x 10" pale grey linen.

For the waistband cut the following:
  x1 piece that measures - 26"x 1½" pale grey linen.

1 Using small scraps of 100% wool, hand dyed felt, cut out the pieces for the toadstool applique.

2 Take the piece of linen for the apron and fold it in half lengthwise. Using the placement guide, position the applique pieces close to the fold and slightly to the left of the centre of the linen.

fold

3 Using tiny applique pins, pin the tiny felt pieces in place on the front of the apron. Open out the apron and using two strands of matching embroidery thread, blanket stitch around the outer edge of all pieces.

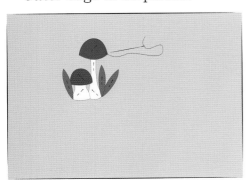

4 Using matching thread to the toadstool stem, stitch long back stitches over the surface of the stem.

5 Using four strands of white embroidery thread, stitch French Knots randomly over the surface of the toadstool caps.

6 Stitch long back stitches through the centre of the leaves.

7 With right sides together, fold the apron in half, lengthwise. Machine stitch the short ends and turn the apron right side out, you now have a raw edge at the top and two neatly stitched sides. Press well.

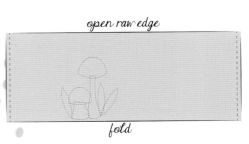

open raw edge

fold

waistband

1 Machine gather along the top raw edge of the apron pull the gathers evenly and lay the apron aside.

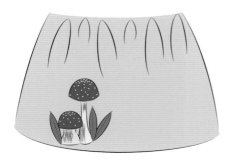

2 Take the waistband piece, fold it in half and finger crease to mark the centre.

fold - finger crease to mark centre

3 With right sides of the band facing the front of the apron, pin the band to the centre top raw edge of the apron, leave approx. 9" of the band over hanging either side of the apron. Machine stitch the band in place, to the front of the apron.

4 Press the band up and over to the inside of the apron and hand stitch the raw edge to the inside of the apron, tucking in the raw ends of the band as you stitch.

shoes

shoes

1 Fold one toe piece in half along the fold line.

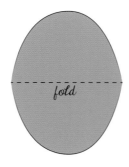

2 Finger press one sole piece in half lengthwise to find the centre.

3 Place the toe piece on top of one sole piece matching the centre crease you made and using two strands of matching embroidery thread, blanket stitch (stitch through all three felt layers) the toe piece to the sole around the toe edge only.

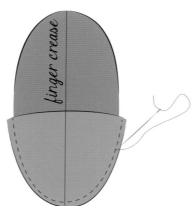

4 Fold the shoe back piece in half lengthwise. Using two strands of matching embroidery thread, blanket stitch the two open curved ends.

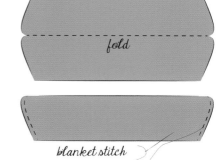

5 Fold the shoe back in half to find the centre, blanket stitch the raw edge in place around the edge at the back of the sole (through all three layers of felt).

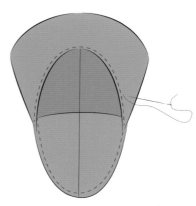

6 Fold the top edges of the shoe back over the top of the toe piece and stitch in place. Stitch a small seed bead in place on the top.

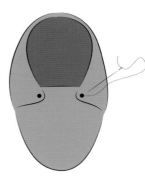

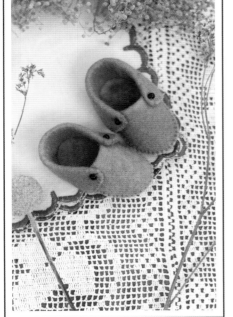

knitted beret with pom pom

beret

Beginning at the band edge
and using the main colour,
cast on 60 stitches.

1 Knit 2, Purl 2, - 7 rows

2 Increase into every stitch –
120 stitches

3 Join on Gold. Beginning
with a knit row, st st 2 rows.

4 Join on Light Blue.
Beginning with knit row, st st
4 rows. Break off Light Blue.

5 Beginning with a knit row,
st st 2 rows Gold. Break off
Gold.

6 Beginning with a knit row,
st st 4 rows of Main Colour.

decreasing

Row 1: Knit 10, k2tog to the end – 110 stitches.

Row 2: Purl

Row 3: Knit 9, k2tog to the end – 100 stitches.

Row 4: Purl

Row 5: Knit 8, k2tog to the end – 90 stitches.

Row 6: Purl

Row 7: Knit 7, k2tog to the end – 80 stitches.

Row 8: Purl - break off Main Colour.

Row 9: Join on Lemon - knit 6, k2tog to the end – 70 stitches.

Row 10: Join on Light Blue - purl

Row 11: Join on Dark Green - knit 5, k2tog to the end – 60 stitches.

Row 12: Using Lemon – purl to the end – break off Lemon.

Row 13: Using Light Blue – knit 4, k2tog to the end – 50 stitches – break off Light Blue.

Row 14: Using Dark Green – purl to the end – break off Dark Green.

Row 15: Join on Main Colour - knit 3, k2tog to the end – 40 stitches.

Row 16: Purl

Row 17: Knit 2, k2tog to the end – 30 stitches.

Row 18: Purl

Row 19: Knit 1, k2tog to the end – 20 stitches.

Row 20: Purl

Row 21: k2 tog to the end. – 10 stitches.

Cut the yarn from the ball, leaving a long length. Thread a bodkin with the length and thread it through the 10 stitches on the knitting needle, remove the knitting needle. Pull up the stitches so they gather into the centre of the top of the beret.

embroidery - duplicate stitch

1 Using one length of desired yarn colour, follow the chart to duplicate stitch (Swiss darning) the extra designs to the beret.

I have used a slightly blunt point needle, as opposed to a sharp needle. A sharp needle can split the fibres of the yarn.

* Block the piece by laying a piece of kitchen towel over it and using a cool iron to steam. Allow the piece to dry.

making up

1 Weave in the yarn at the ends of all the rows.

2 Thread the long length of Main Colour yarn at the top of the beret on to a bodkin. Mattress stitch the row ends together all the way down to the band. Fasten off.

pom pom

1 Using a 2.5" (6cm) Pom Pom maker and Red yarn follow the instructions on the pack to make a tight pom pom.

2 Leave a long tail of yarn for stitching the pom pom to the beret. Trim the rest of the pom pom so you have a nice, neat, trim ball.

3 Stitch the pom pom to the top of the beret.

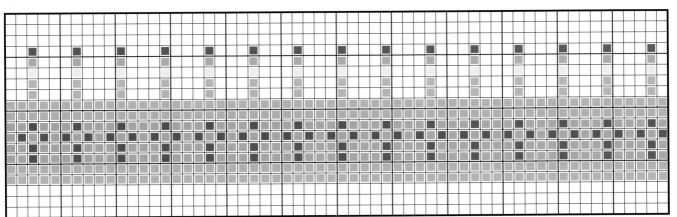

pantaloons

pantaloons

1 Press under a neat hem on both pieces along the bottom edge. Machine stitch in place.

2 Take the length of decorative ribbon/braid, cut it in half and top stitch it in place along the bottom edge.

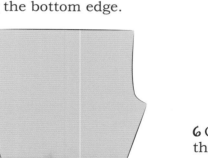

3 With right sides together, stitch down both gusset seams.

4 Bring the gusset seams into the middle so they are even. Now stitch the inner leg seams.

5 Turn under a neat hem around the top waist edge and machine stitch in place, leaving a small gap for threading the elastic. Turn the pantaloons right side out and press.

gap for elastic

6 Cut approx. 15cm (6") thin elastic. Attach a small safety pin to one end of the elastic and thread the elastic through the waistband. Stitch the ends of the elastic together, then close the opening in the waistband.

knitted apples

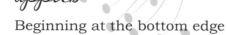

apples

Beginning at the bottom edge and cast on 15 stitches.

1 Purl 1 row.

2 Increase into every stitch – 30 stitches.

3 Beginning with a purl row, st st 12 rows.

4 Purl 2tog to the end –15 stitches.

leaves

1 Place two leaves together and using a ¼ inch seam allowance on your sewing machine, stitch the two leaf shapes together. Stitch down the centre of each leaf.

2 Use pinking shears to carefully cut around the outer edge of each leaf. Make one leaf per apple.

making up

1 Cut the yarn from the ball, leaving a long length. Thread a bodkin with the length and thread it through the 15 stitches on the knitting needle, remove the knitting needle. Pull up the stitches so they gather into the centre of the apple.

2 With wrong sides together, mattress stitch the row ends together all the way down, fasten off. Stuff the apple until firm. Approx 13cm (5.5") circumference.

3 Gather around the open edge and pull up the gathers tight and fasten off.

4 Thread a sharp needle with a long length of brown Perle thread. Place the point of one leaf on top of the centre of the apple, push the needle through the point of the leaf and down into the apple, right through to the bottom (leaving a small tail of thread at the top).

5 Thread a small black seed bead on to the end of the thread at the bottom of the apple.

6 Now push the needle up through the centre of the apple and come up and out at the top, pulling the apple a tiny bit to make an indent in the bottom of the apple. (The seed bead with now sit in the indent in the bottom of the apple).

7 Push the needle down through the centre of the apple a second time, leaving a loop of thread at the top. Repeat a third time leaving a second loop at the top.

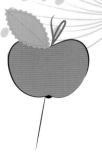

8 Finally bring the needle up to the top of the apple, you should have two loops of thread and two tails of thread.

9 Remove the needle. Tie the loops in a knot to secure.

apple bushel

YOU WILL NEED

- 42cm x 26cm (16.5"x 10") 'Cocoa' wool felt for the bushel base and handles

- 30cm x 10cm (11"x 10") 'Oak' wool felt for the bushel bands

- Embroidery thread to match the felt

- Sewing machine thread to match the felt

- Wonder Clips

- Contrasting thread for tacking

- General sewing supplies

* 5mm (¼") seam allowance included

* templates on page 127

bushel

1 Trace and cut out the pattern piece for the bushel very carefully.

2 Fold the piece of felt in half and pin the bushel pattern piece on top of the folded felt at regular intervals so it is securely and accurately in place.

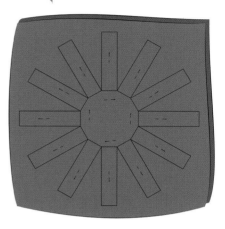

3 Using a sewing machine thread to match the felt, and the pattern piece as a guide, stitch around the outside edge of the bushel pattern piece, as close to the pattern as possible.

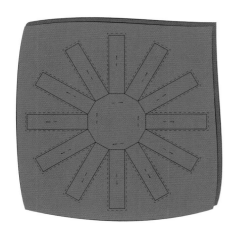

4 Remove the pattern piece and using a sharp pair of scissors, carefully cut out the bushel, leaving a small seam allowance as you cut along all the lines of sewing.

bands

1 Cut four bands for the bushel in a contrasting colour felt that measure 1"x 11.5" (2.5cm x 29cm)

1" x 11.5" (2.5cm x 29cm)

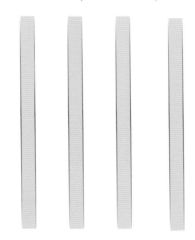

2 Bring the short ends together on one of the bands to form a 'ring' and using a ¼" seam allowance, stitch the short ends together.

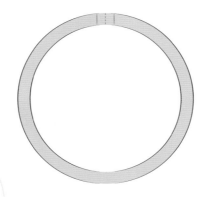

3 With wrong sides together, fold the band in half lengthwise and top stitch. Repeat with two of the other bands, leaving one unstitched at the stage.

4 Take one of the stitched bands, beginning at the bottom and on the outside of the bushel, weave it in and out of the spokes of the bushel. Tack it in place with contrasting thread just to hold it in place.

tack to hold

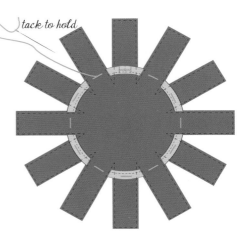

5 Repeat weaving with the second band but this time begin on the inside of the bushel, tacking it in place just on top of the first band.

6 Repeat again with the third band, again on the outside of the bushel.

7 Take the last band, bring the short ends together to form a ring and using a ¼" seam allowance, stitch the short end together.

3 Fold the ring in half wrong sides together over the top edge of the bushel. Use Wonder Clips to hold it in place as you blanket stitch the band to the top edge of the bushel. Remove the tacking stitches.

handles

1 Cut two handles that measure 1"x 3" (2.5cm x 8cm) Fold each on in half lengthwise and top stitch.

2 Stitch the short ends of the handles in place on either side of the bushel as pictured. Stitch a tiny red seed bead to each end of the handles.

stitch

1" x 3" (2.5cm x 8cm)

Damson

fox satchel

YOU WILL NEED

- 28cm x 26cm (11"x 10") 'Mallee' wool felt for the satchel
- 28cm x 26cm (11"x 10") fabric for the satchel
- 9cm x 7cm (3.5"x 3") 'Ecru' wool felt for face applique
- Small scrap of 'Coal Black' wool felt for the eyes
- Black embroidery thread
- Ecru embroidery thread
- x1 Small snap/press stud
- Sewing machine thread to match the felt
- Tiny applique pins (optional)
- General sewing supplies

* 5mm (¼") seam allowance included

* templates on page 124

fox satchel

1 Place the two fox face applique pieces in place on the felt satchel piece. Using two strands of matching embroidery thread, blanket stitch around the inside curved edge.

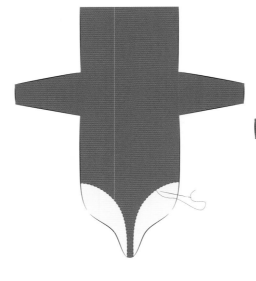

2 Cut out two tiny dots from black felt for the eyes. Place them as indicated on the face of the fox. Using two strands of black embroidery thread, blanket stitch around the tiny dots. (You could also stitch French Knots for the eyes using 4 strands of black embroidery thread, if you prefer.)

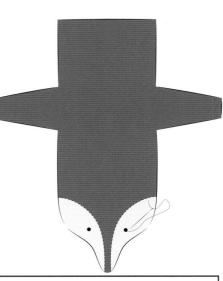

3 Using two strands of a slightly darker colour thread than you chose for the fox. Stitch short back stitches in place as indicated, randomly over the surface of the fox head and down the middle of the nose.

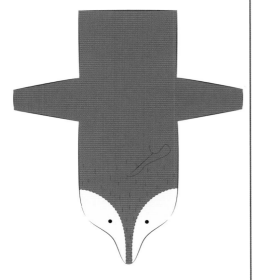

4 With right sides facing, place the two satchel pieces together. Machine stitch all the way around the outer edge, leaving open where indicated at the square end. Clip the corners, turn right side out and press well. Hand stitch the opening closed.

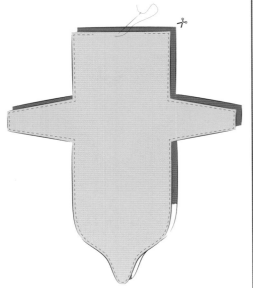

5 Using two strands of black embroidery thread, stitch a few backstitches over each other on the tip of the nose. Pass the thread back through the stitches and fasten off.

7 Stitch one side of a small black snap/press stud to the under side of the nose and the remaining side of the snap to the front of the satchel to fasten.

ears

1 Place two ears together and using a tiny 3mm seam allowance, machine stich all the way around each ear, leaving open where indicated along the bottom edge.

strap

1 Cut a piece of felt for the strap that measures 10" x 1" (26cm x 2.5cm) Fold it in half lengthwise and machine top stitch.

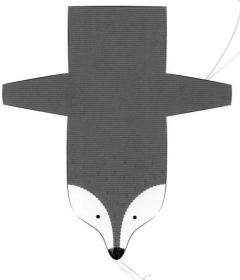

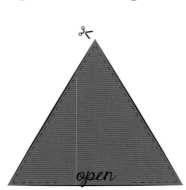

10" x 1" (26cm x 2.5cm)

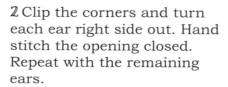

2 Hand stitch the ends of the strap to either side of the satchel.

6 Bring together one side of the satchel with the square end and hand stitch them together, repeat with the remaining side. Now stitch the side to the front face end of the satchel. The face of the fox will then be folded over the front as the 'flap' of the bag.

2 Clip the corners and turn each ear right side out. Hand stitch the opening closed. Repeat with the remaining ears.

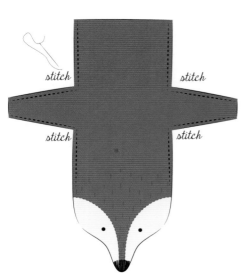

3 Pin each ear in place as indicated, on top of the head. Hand stitch them in place.

89

long sleeve blouse

~YOU WILL NEED~

. 45cm x 34cm (18"x 13.5")
  fabric for blouse
. 15cm (6") piece of thin
  elastic
. Sewing machine thread to
  match the fabric
. x2 Small vintage/novelty
  buttons
. Perle thread for the button
  loops
. General sewing supplies

* 5mm (¼") seam
  allowance included
* templates on page 112

Make in the same way as for Chamomile's short sleeve blouse on page 28, noting modified sleeve instructions.

sleeves

1 Press under a neat hem on each sleeve approx. 1.5cm (½") wide to make the elastic casing.

2 Continue in the same way as for Chamomile's short sleeve blouse.

britches

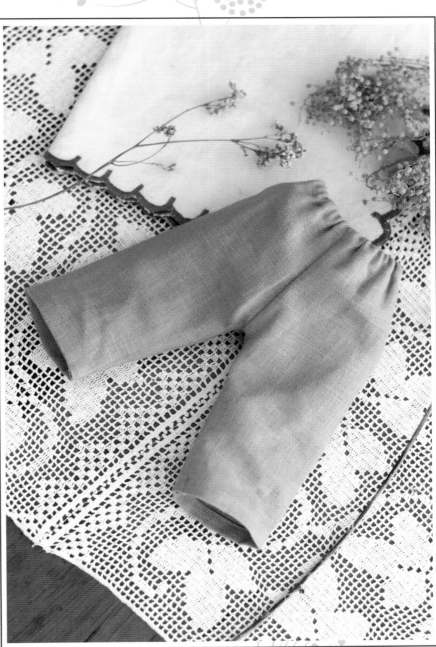

Make in the same way as
for Laurel's pantaloons on
page 72.

knitted dress

Beginning at the upper edge and using the main colour, cast on 46 stitches.

1 Garter stitch 11 row.

2 Increase into every stitch – 92 stitches.

3 Beginning with a knit row, st st 40 rows.

4 Garter stitch 6 rows.

Cast off.

embroidery - duplicate stitch

1 Using one length of desired yarn colour, follow the chart to duplicate stitch (Swiss darning) the extra designs to the dress.

I have used a slightly blunt point needle, as opposed to a sharp needle. A sharp needle can split the fibres of the yarn.

* Block the piece by laying a piece of kitchen towel over it and using a cool iron to steam. Allow the piece to dry.

making up

1 Weave in the yarn at the ends of all the rows.

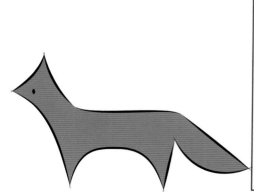

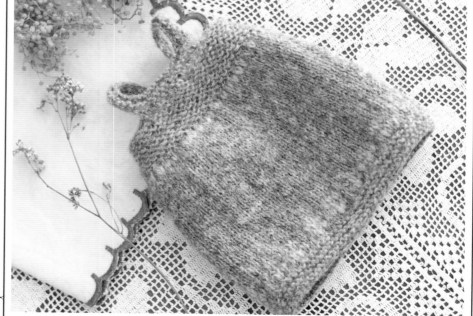

2 Thread a long length of Main Colour yarn on to a bodkin. Mattress stitch the Stocking Stitch row ends together all the way down to the bottom. Leave the 11 rows of Garter Stitch on the upper edge unstitched. Fasten off.

button loop

Finger knit (or crochet) a 3cm (1¼) long chain. With the back of the dress facing you, stitch the ends of the button loop to the top right corner of the upper edge Garter Stitch rows. Stitch a small button in place opposite the loop.

strap

1 Using Main Colour, cast on 50 stitches.

2 Garter Stitch 2 rows, cast off.

3 Find the centre of the strap and the centre front of the dress. Stitch the strap across the top of the upper edge of the dress approx. 6cm (2½").

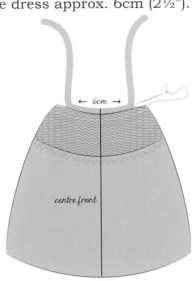

4 Stitch the ends of the strap to the back of the upper edge of the dress near the loop and button.

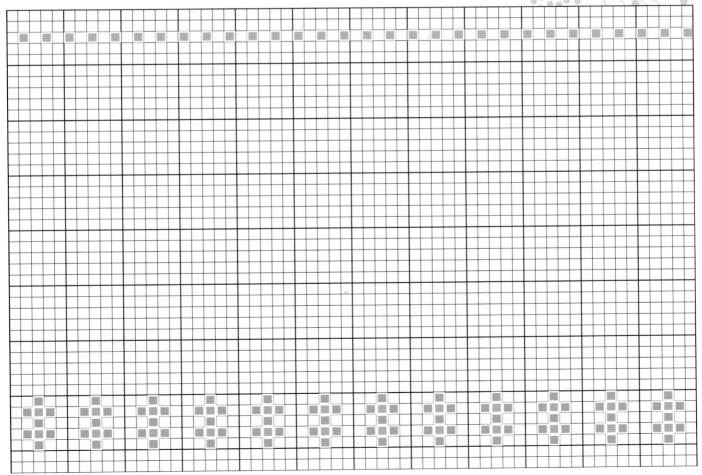

templates actual size

moccasins

moccasins

1 Finger press one sole piece
in half lengthwise. Finger
press one moccasin toe piece
in half lengthwise also.

2 Place one toe piece on top of
one sole piece matching the
centre crease you made and
using two strands of matching
embroidery thread, blanket
stitch the toe piece to the sole
around the toe edge only.

3 Repeat step 1 with the
moccasin back and blanket
stitch it in place along the
bottom edge around the back
of the sole. Repeat all steps to
make the second moccasin.

4 Make a small hole in the back piece in the top inside corner of each moccasin. Blanket stitch around the outer edge of the hole to strengthen.

5 Stitch a tiny shank button in place opposite the hole on the other curved edge of the back piece.

6 Cut approx. 25cm (10") of cotton twine. Place a knot in each end of the twine and fold the twine in half. Thread it through the hole in the moccasin and back through the loop to hold it in place.

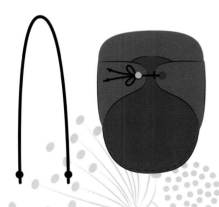

7 Place the moccasins on the doll's feet. Tie each moccasin in place by tying a bow in the twine and anchoring it to the shank button.

knitted fallow deer hat

YOU WILL NEED

abbreviations

st st = stocking stitch

k2tog = knit two stitches together

p2tog = purl 2 together

* These decrease methods are described in detail on the website bellow:

www.newstitchaday.com

hat

. 3.25mm (3¼) knitting needles

. 4 ply yarn:

Hat:
    Yellow Ochre - 230

Spots:
    Natural White – 104

. Bodkin/Tapestry needle

flowers

. 6cm x 4cm (2.5″ x 1.5″) 'Tasman' wool felt

. 6cm x 4cm (2.5″ x 1.5″) 'Coral' wool a

. Embroidery thread to match the felts

. x4 Black seed beads

. General sewing supplies

* *flower templates on page 123*

hat

Beginning at the face edge, cast on 58 stitches.

Garter Stitch 6 rows, slipping the first stitch knit wise on every row.

* Begin Stocking Stitch

1 Slip the first stitch knit wise, knit to the end of the row.

2 Slip the first stitch knit wise, knit 2, purl to the last 3 stitches, knit 3.

* Repeat these two rows 11 more times.

shaping the back

1 Slip the first stitch knit wise, knit 18, k2tog 10 times, knit 19
– 48 stitches.

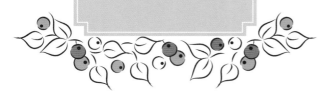

2 Garter stitch 5 rows, slipping the first stitch knit wise on every row.

3 Slip first stitch knit wise, knit 13, k2tog 10 times, knit 14 – 38 stitches.

4 Garter stitch 3 rows, slipping the first stitch knit wise on every row.

5 Slip the first stitch knit wise, knit 8, k2tog 10 times, knit 9 – 28 stitches.

Cast off.

* Block the piece by laying a piece of kitchen towel over it and using a cool iron to steam. Allow the piece to dry.

making up

6 Thread the length of yarn on to a bodkin. Fold the cast off edge in half and mattress stitch across the cast off edge. Weave in the ends of any remaining yarn. Fasten off.

ears

Make two in total

Cast on 12 stitches.

1 Beginning with a knit row, st st 10 rows.

* Continue in stocking stitch

2 k2tog at the beginning of the next row.

3 p2tog at the beginning of the next row.

* Repeat these two rows 5 more times until 2 stitches remain.

4 Increase 1 stitch at the beginning of the next 10 rows – 12 stitches.

Stocking stitch 10 rows.

Cast off.

making up

1 With wrong side of the piece together, fold the piece in half. Mattress stitch the row ends together.

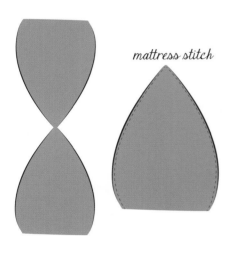

mattress stitch

2 Fold the ear in half and place a few stitches in the straight edge to hold.

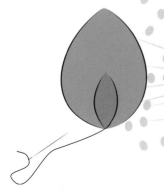

3 Stitch the ears to either side of the hat.

spots

Make 5 in total

1 Using Natural White yarn, cast on 6 stitches.

2 Cut the yarn leaving a long tail. Thread the yarn on to a bodkin and thread each stitch on to the bodkin, remove the knitting needle.

3 Pull up the stitches firmly, so they form a small bunch/circle. Stitch the spot on to the top of the hat.

twisted tie

Make two in total

1 Cut two 60cm (23.5") lengths of matching yarn.

2 Tape the two ends to a tabletop and twist the yarn until it is very firm.

3 Remove from the tabletop and fold the piece in half and let it twist back on itself. Smooth it out and knot the ends together.

4 Stitch each folded end to the front corners of the hat.

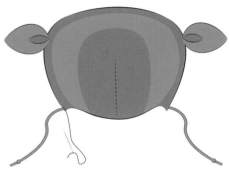

flowers

1 Cut two flowers for each ear.

    X2 Tasman

    X2 Coral

2 Fold each flower in quarters and add a few tiny stitches on the fold to hold in place.

stitch

3 Stitch each flower to the front of each ear with a tiny black seed bead in the centre of each flower.

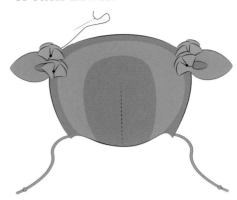

Templates

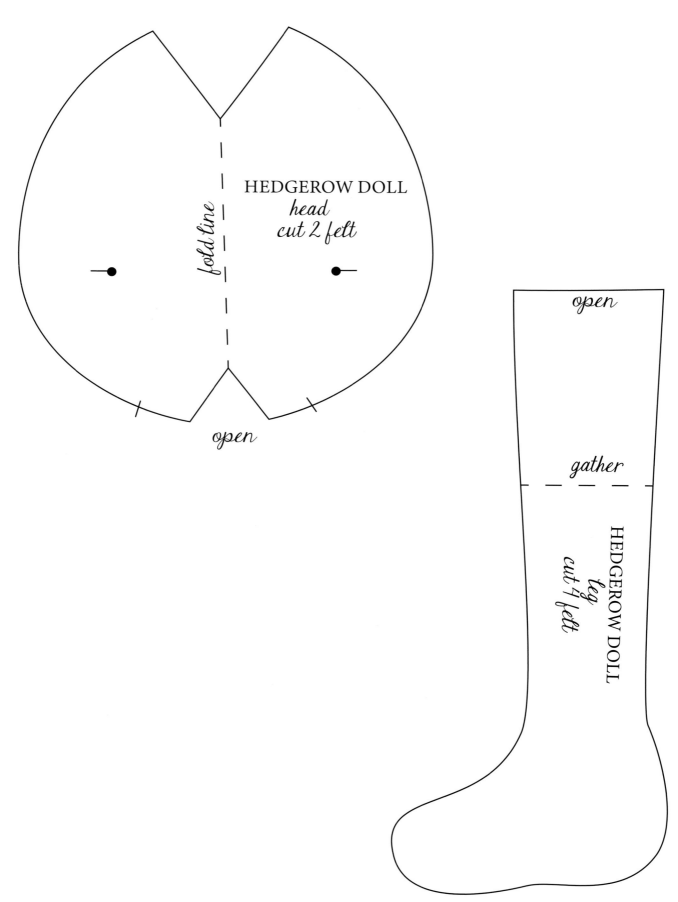

HEDGEROW DOLL
head
cut 2 felt

fold line

open

open

gather

HEDGEROW DOLL
leg
cut 4 felt

templates actual size

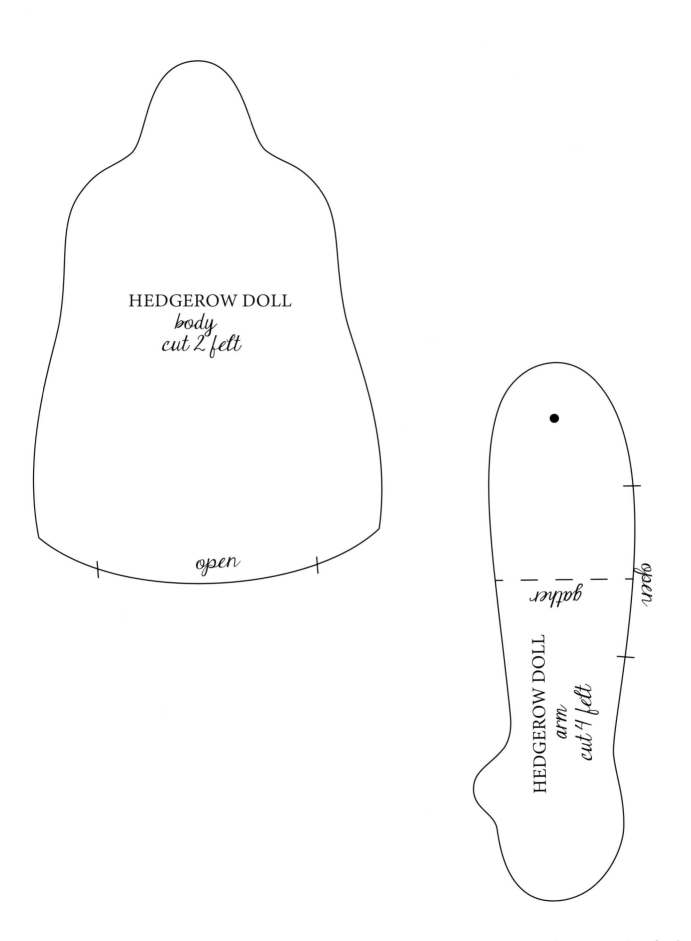

HEDGEROW DOLL
body
cut 2 felt

open

HEDGEROW DOLL
arm
cut 4 felt

gather

open

templates actual size

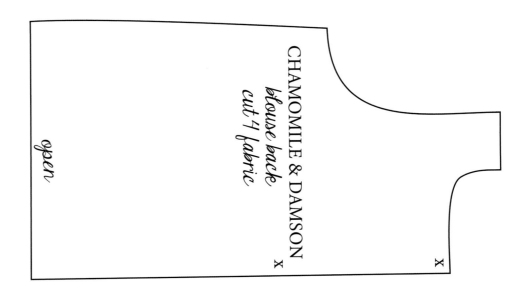

CHAMOMILE & DAMSON
blouse back
cut 4 fabric

open

x

x

CHAMOMILE & DAMSON
blouse front
cut 2 fabric

open

templates actual size

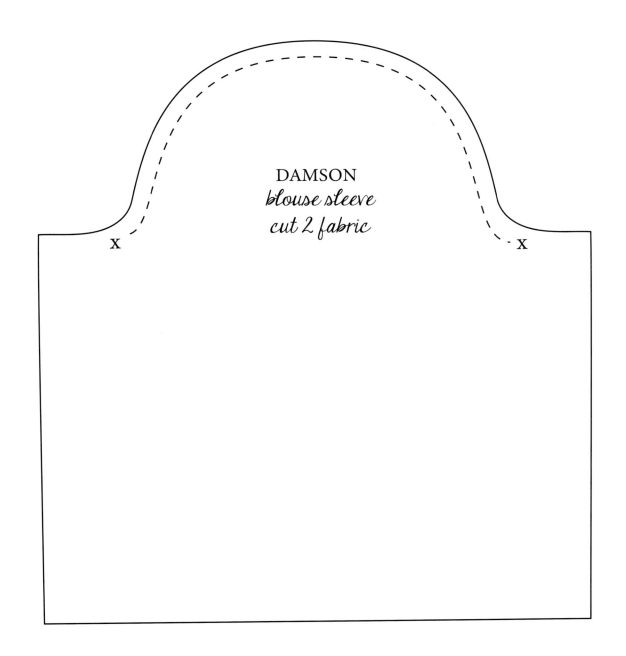

DAMSON
blouse sleeve
cut 2 fabric

X   X

templates actual size

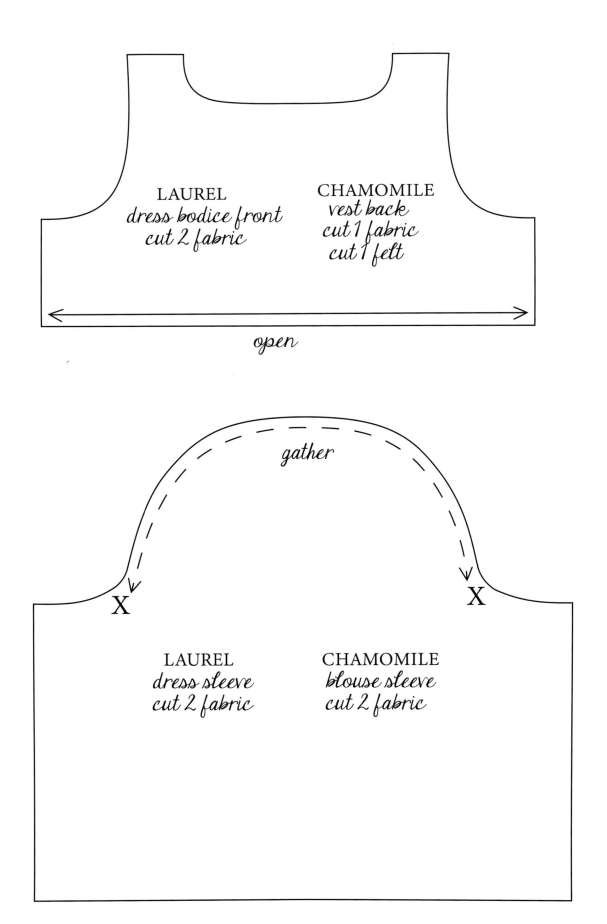

LAUREL
dress bodice front
cut 2 fabric

CHAMOMILE
vest back
cut 1 fabric
cut 1 felt

open

gather

X   X

LAUREL
dress sleeve
cut 2 fabric

CHAMOMILE
blouse sleeve
cut 2 fabric

templates actual size

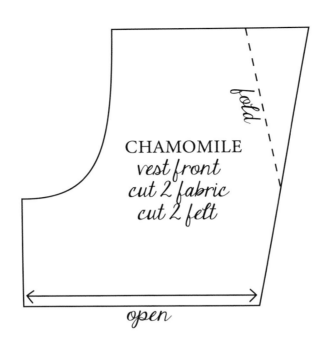

CHAMOMILE
vest front
cut 2 fabric
cut 2 felt

fold

open

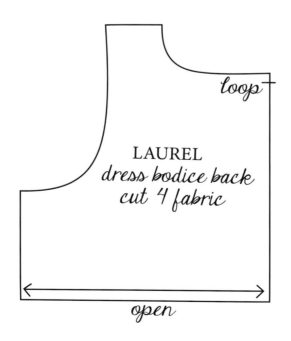

loop

LAUREL
dress bodice back
cut 4 fabric

open

templates actual size

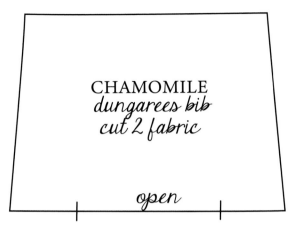

CHAMOMILE
dungarees bib
cut 2 fabric

open

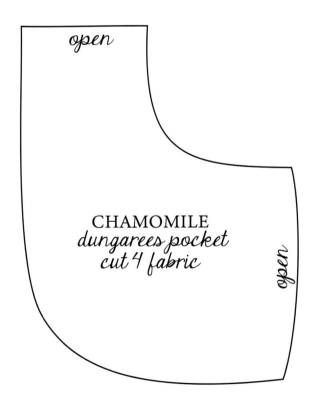

open

CHAMOMILE
dungarees pocket
cut 4 fabric

open

LAUREL
apple leaf
cut 10 felt

templates actual size

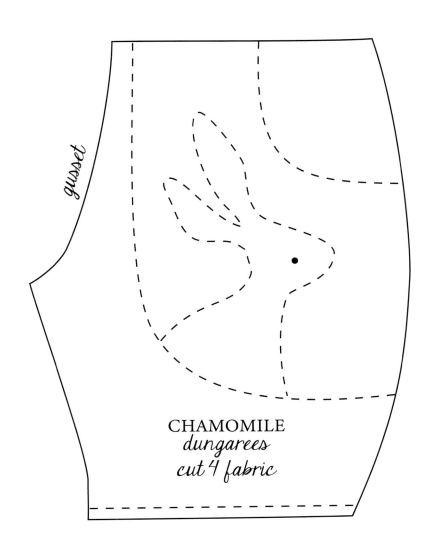

gusset

CHAMOMILE
dungarees
cut 4 fabric

RABBIT
applique
cut 2 felt

templates actual size

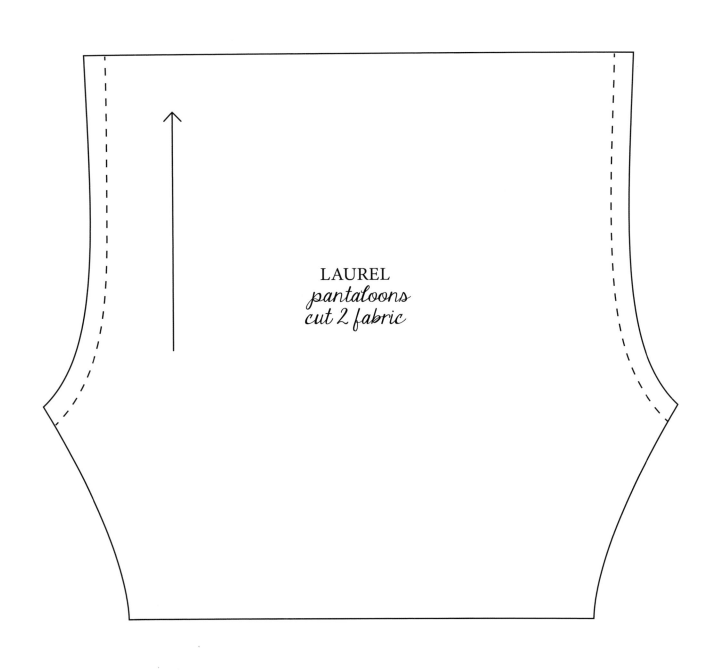

LAUREL
pantaloons
cut 2 fabric

templates actual size

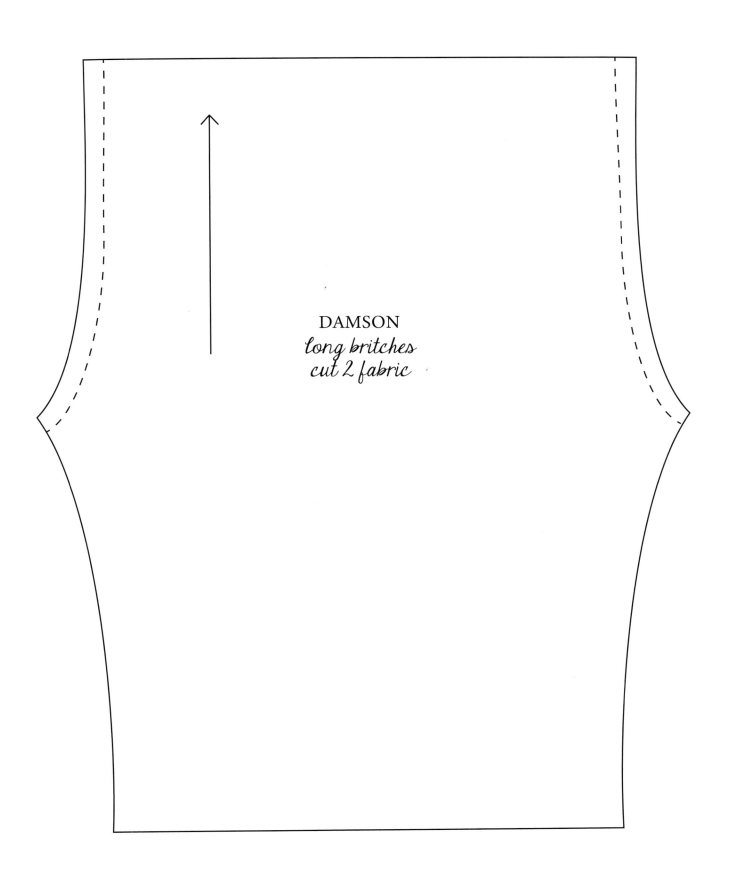

DAMSON
long britches
cut 2 fabric

templates actual size

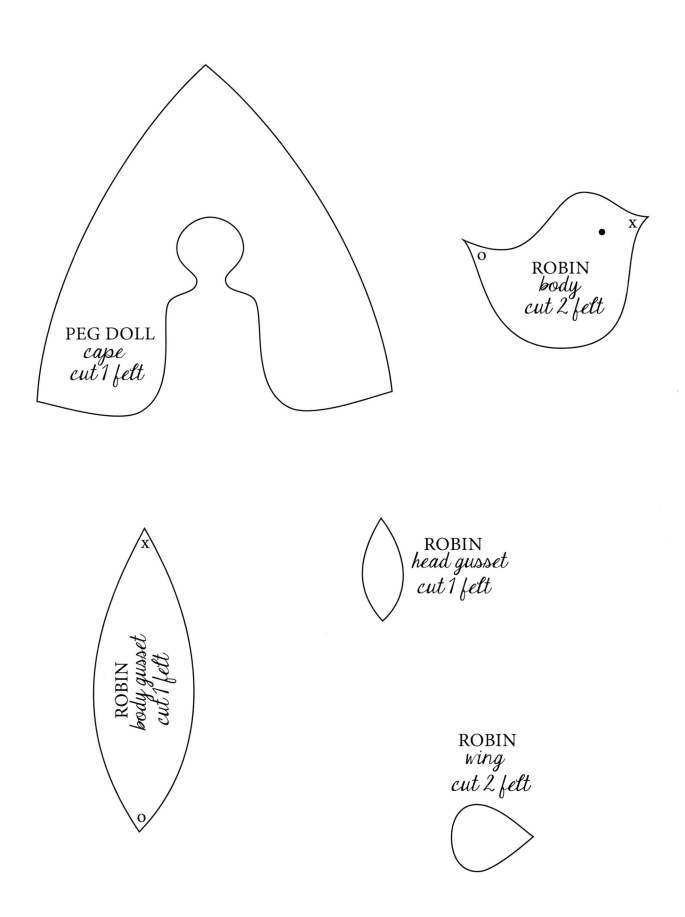

PEG DOLL
cape
cut 1 felt

ROBIN
body
cut 2 felt

O   X

ROBIN
head gusset
cut 1 felt

X

ROBIN
body gusset
cut 1 felt

O

ROBIN
wing
cut 2 felt

templates actual size

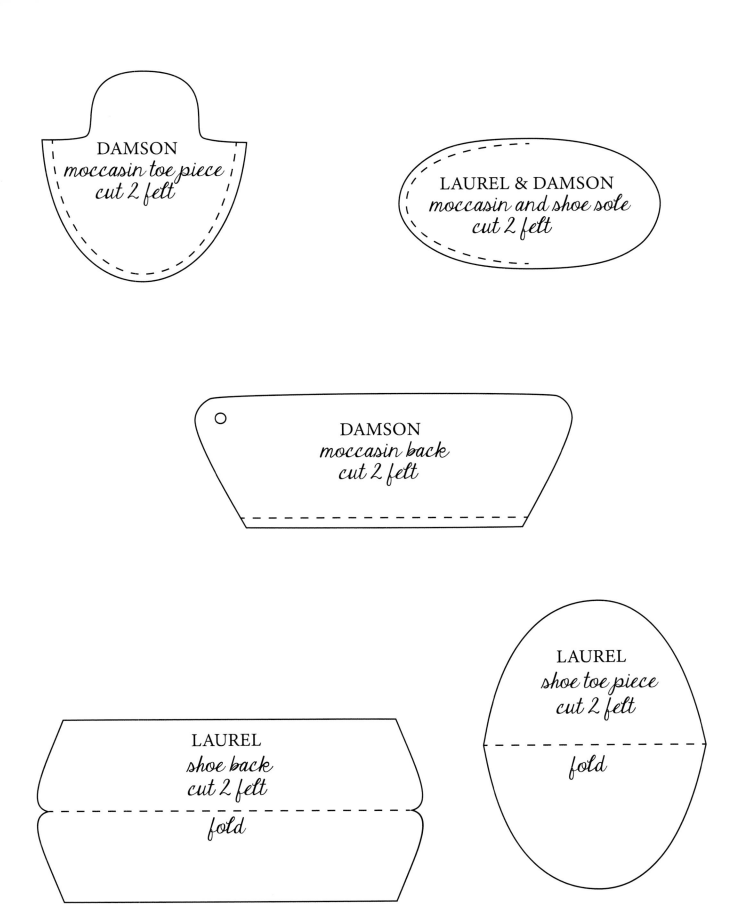

DAMSON
*moccasin toe piece
cut 2 felt*

LAUREL & DAMSON
*moccasin and shoe sole
cut 2 felt*

DAMSON
*moccasin back
cut 2 felt*

LAUREL
*shoe back
cut 2 felt*

fold

LAUREL
*shoe toe piece
cut 2 felt*

fold

templates actual size

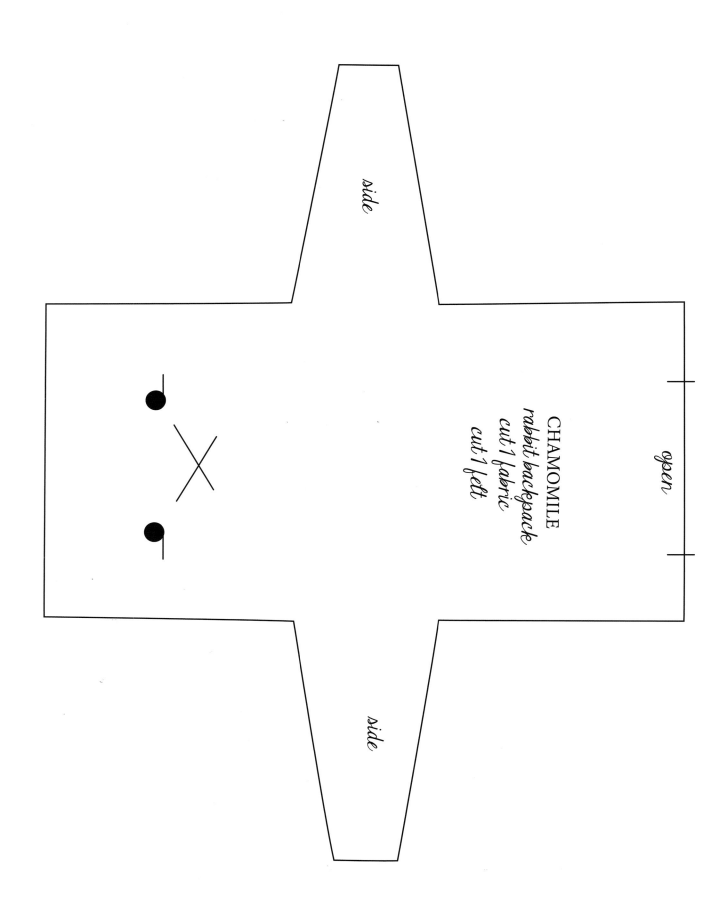

side

CHAMOMILE
rabbit backpack
cut 1 fabric
cut 1 felt

open

side

templates actual size

DAMSON
fallow deer hat flower
cut 4 felt

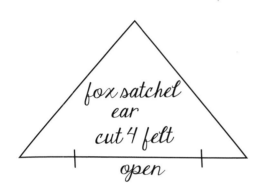

fox satchel
ear
cut 4 felt
open

open

rabbit backpack ear
cut 4 felt

templates actual size

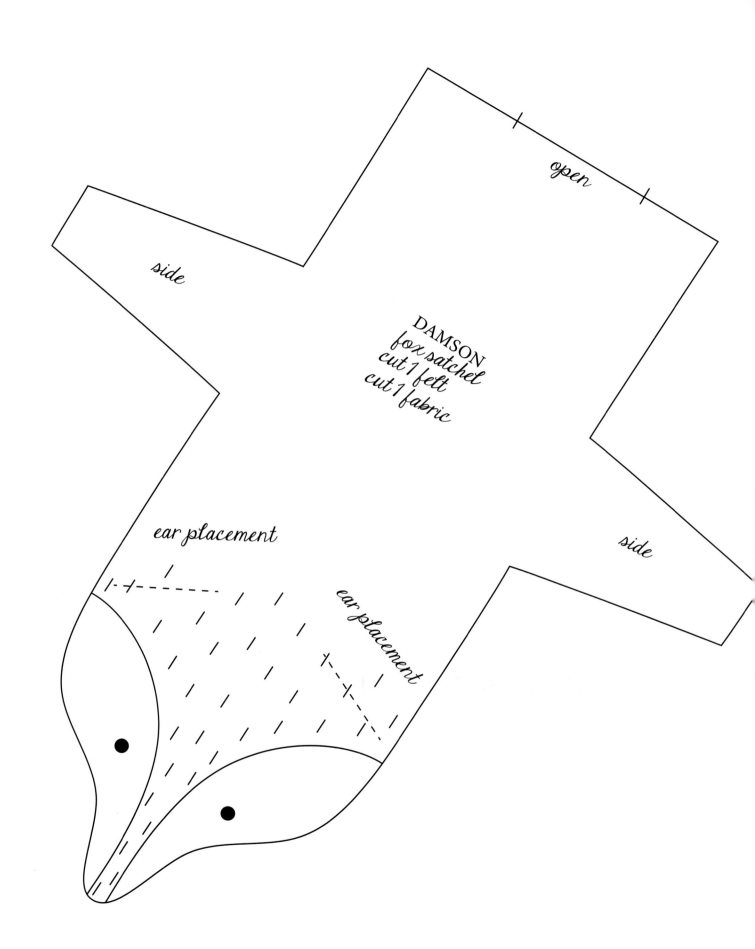

open

side

DAMSON
fox satchel
cut 1 felt
cut 1 fabric

side

ear placement

ear placement

templates actual size

eye cut 2 felt

*fox satchel
face applique
cut 2 felt*

TOADSTOOL APPLIQUE
placement guide

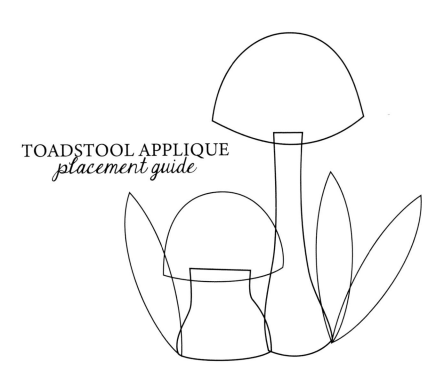

templates actual size

LAUREL APRON TOADSTOOL APPLIQUE PIECES

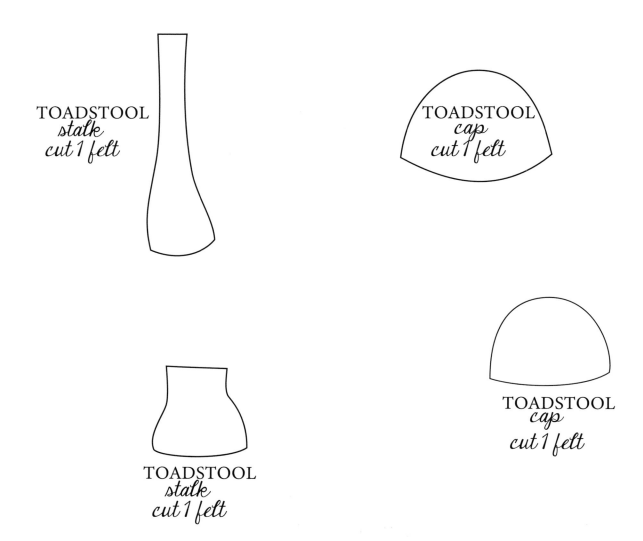

TOADSTOOL
stalk
cut 1 felt

TOADSTOOL
cap
cut 1 felt

TOADSTOOL
stalk
cut 1 felt

TOADSTOOL
cap
cut 1 felt

TOADSTOOL
leaf
cut 3 felt

templates actual size

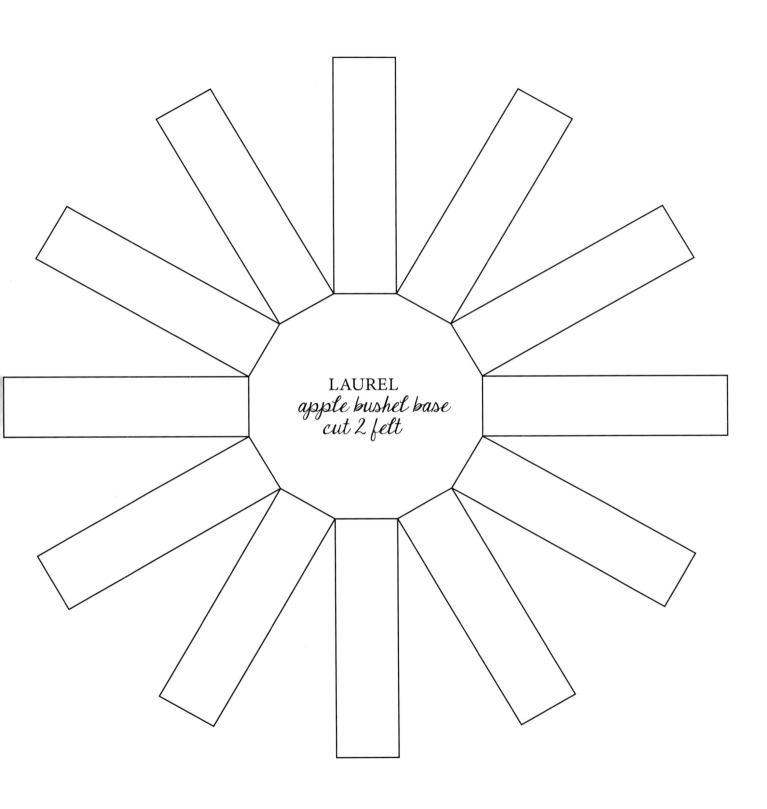

LAUREL
apple bushel base
cut 2 felt

templates actual size

Suppliers

felt

Winterwood
www.winterwoodtoys.com.au

fabric

L'uccello
www.luccello.com.au

linen

The Fabric Store
www.wearethefabricstore.com

eyes

Bear Essence
www.bearessence.com.au

yarn

Jamieson's of Shetland
www.jamiesonsofshetland.co.uk

embroidery thread

Cosmo Embroidery Thread
www.etsy.com

buttons

Vintage
www.etsy.com and my own collection